Good Grief's Guide to Healing

Elgina Bullock-Smith

ROYSTON
Publishing

© Copyright – 2020

All Rights Reserved. No part of this book may be reproduced, stored in a retrieval system, or transmitted by any means without the written permission of the author.

Cover Design Layout: Elite Book Covers
Back Cover Family Photo: Ty Lockhart Photography

ISBN-13: 978-1-951941-50-5

Additional Editing Services by: Terrence Bullock and Billistris Minor

Disclaimer: The information in this book is purely for educational purposes to assist families in their time of bereavement. In no way is the author or publisher endorsing or certifying any of the organizations or companies services but striving to provide information, education and options for families to consider. Please visit all websites, contact the organizations directly via phone and/or email for the most current and up to date information and resources to help you make the best possible decision for you, your family and your love ones. Due to the COVID-19 Global Pandemic, please contact the organization, business and/or visit their website regarding their current and most up to date protocols, practices and procedures for doing business and engaging with these entities.

Other Books by Elgina Bullock-Smith:
Morning After Mourning which is the accompanying book to this workbook that tells her story of loss and grief. Available by email at mrs.smithelgina@gmail.com

Printed in the United States of America

Dedication

This book is dedicated to my spiritual (midwife)
Janeen Drake, the pastor over New Beginnings Empowerment temple.

Thank you for allowing me the space to birth and activate my life's calling. I have been blessed to sow and grow into ministry through becoming spiritually empowered under your leadership!

{Pamper Me Pretty} is more than a yearly gathering of women. It's a much needed, mighty movement ministry, that God has allowed me to be a mantle carrier. No, I didn't start this journey but I'm willing to see it through .wherever God leads me to I'll go! I'm forever grateful for your eternal love and support.

Special Acknowledgements

The late Mother Elizabeth Kelly

Pastor Susan Bradley

Minister Monique Davis Williams

Rev. Dr. Yuvanne Wilson

Jennifer Stanton, Norton's Hospital, she is a heaven sent friend.

Pastor Yvonne McCoy, founder of Oasis Wellness Center and all the active board members. Tuniscia Okeke, my life coach

Thanks to my family for your support personal inputs & interviews:

My husband Anthony Smith Sr.
My mother Elder Jeanine Lee
My grandma pastor Julie Grice
My daughter Danielle Gartin
My daughter Lanyia Smith
My sister- in -love Iishia Bullock and brother, Elgin Bullock
My brother Justin Bullock
My brother Cameron Bullock

My dear friend Artrice Hansberry ministry and community ambassador
Camp EverGreen from Hospice

Table of Contents

Dedication	iii
Special Acknowledgements	v
We Have All Lost Something	1
Rest Assured with Insurance	5
Living Witness	17
Self-Care is Like Medicine to a Mourner	19
Planning the Funeral Arrangements	21
Cremation vs. Burial	23
Premonition Intuition Dreams	31
Who is a Grieving Mother?	37
I Live for Us Both Now	39
Top 10 Things You Should Never Say to a Mourning Mother!	41
My Grief Rights	43
Caution I'm Fragile and Mending from Mourning.....	45
Being Married and Mourning	49
An Advocating Voice for the Child(ren) Left Behind, with the Mourning Parent(s)	53
Celebrating the Holidays	57
Let Me Feed Your Broken Heart With Some Soul Food	59
Counseling for Grieving Couples & Families	71
Do You Remember the Story of Jonah?	75

Your Loved Ones Belongings and Inventory	77
Attitude of Gratitude	79
Monthly Inspirational Scripture and Reflection	81
Growing Through Year 1	109
Growing Through Year 3	111
Growing Through Year 5	113
References	115
Books for Motivation and Inspiration	116
Special Thank You's	117
Pictorial Gallery	118
Reflection	121

We Have All Lost Something

We have All lost something or someone. This is just an exercise to show how grief and lost have different emotional values to us all. Grief can't be measured and often the loss of something you valued is hard to explain but a loved one is the greatest loss to bear.

What all have you lost? Circle your truth. (Personal) loss

Mother	Father	Child
Husband	Wife	Grandmother
Grandfather	Brother	Sister
Aunt	Uncle	Cousin
Teacher	A Close Friend	A Neighbor
A Pet		

Loss (Opportunity)

School Date	Winning lottery ticket
Trip out of town	Getting married
Having a baby	Money
A Bid	Chance to Sign a deal or contract
Moving	Meeting someone special
Speaking to a stranger	Asking for help
A promotion	Job

(Things) You've Lost

Keys	Credit cards	Clothing
Shoes	House	Car Ring
Cell Phone	Memories	Friendship
Homework	Grocery list	Favorite book
Self-esteem	Weight	Lighter
Recipe	Respect	Hope

This activity was just to show you that we should value life and not stuff because we were given this life and free will.

The truth is that the stuff we paid for is depreciating in value every day.
So, appreciate the priceless people in your life more than the stuff you'll soon be throwing away. We all just get the one life to live so take each day to appreciate what we've been given.

Reflection

Rest Assured With Insurance

Put your mind to rest knowing you have everything covered just in case.

There's a million insurance companies and different types and coverages in their insurance policies.

The 6 Best Whole Life Insurance Policies of 2020 were listed as:

- New York Life: Best Overall
- Northwestern Mutual: Best for Dividends
- State Farm: Best for Bundling
- Mass Mutual: Best for Cash Values
- Guardian Life: Best for Estate Planning
- Mutual of Omaha: Best for Child Life Insurance

Now you still have to be careful choosing a policy. Make sure you read & ask questions about everything you don't understand.

Confusion generally comes into play when an agent works the policy to fit your pockets allotted offering and not the actual security blanket needed to protect & cover your life's business. Having an insurance policy in place ensures your family that you'll be able to run smoothly in case of an unexpected Emergency.

What I mean by this is you need to make sure you understand the breakdown behind giving an insurance company your family's business. Believe me cheap doesn't always make the policy better. Getting a full understanding is priceless.

Question: What are the benefits of having a whole life policy?

Answer-Whole Life Insurance Is A Permanent Policy Guaranteeing Protection

For your Family. It has Cash Value. You are Eligible For Dividends.

You can borrow from your policy to Care For Special Needs. You can use it as a Plan For Retirement. It can be used in emergencies But most importantly it's in place to Plan For The Unexpected Death Benefits.

Compare – What is the difference between whole life and a term policy?

Answer - The primary difference between whole life and term insurance is the duration of the policy. A whole life insurance policy ends when you die, while a term life insurance policy lasts for a pre-determined period of time. Another important distinction of a whole life policy is the cash value that accumulates over time.

Don't wait to find out about the fine print behind having your children covered under a child term rider on your policy it may not be worth it in the long run.

In summary, a Child Rider on your insurance policy means the following:

- A Child rider is an insured child covered under an insured parent policy. Only children 18 and under at issue can be insured under a child rider.
- Child riders guarantee the future insurability of the insured's children until the conversion period expires.
- Child riders automatically cover any future children you may have.
- Child riders insure the child up to maximum age (typically 18 - 23 years old), or until the parent stops paying the premium, or until the parent's term policy is up, or until the parent turns 65, whichever comes first.
- Child riders need to be converted into a permanent policy before maximum age.

At conversion, the parent can transfer ownership to child or continue to own it themselves. Typically, a single child rider will cover all of the children in your household. Each insurance company will decide how long a child is covered, but most typically cover children starting at 15 days old and ending sometime between age 18 and 22, with most ending at 18.

10 Things You Should Know Before Purchasing Life Insurance

For all of your insurance needs, Talk to an insurance agent. He or she can help you evaluate your insurance needs and give you information about available policies that can fit your family needs.

Some questions and/or issues to consider:

- **Decide How Much Coverage You Need**
- **Assess Your Current Life Insurance Policy**
- **Compare The Different Kinds of Insurance Policies**
- **Be Sure You Can Afford the Premium Payments**
- **Have an Insurance Agent Help You Evaluate the Future of Your Policy**
- **Keep Your Current Policy**
- **Understand Renewal Policies**
- **Read Your Policy Carefully**
- **Review Your Life Insurance Program Every Few Years**

Now let's address the issues No one wants to talk about The Uninsured…

What happens when you don't have the coverage?

This could End in either 4 ways

1. **The Family Feuds**

   Most often the family draws together to help bury their loved one this would seem to be a kind gesture however oftentimes borrowing money follows with the family feuding and Disputing and Ultimately loss of support completely leaving the grieving family at odds with one another.

2. **The Bailout Bait**

   There's always a bank that will allow you to take out a personal loan which will depend on your credit score. However, you will never break even this method. A personal loan will leaves you with grief loss and a monthly extra cost.

3. **The famous *Go Fund Me* account**

   This is known best for publicly announcing that you're requesting and soliciting the help of almost anyone willing to help you. All people have to do is see the post through social media and feel compelled to donate.

   Unfortunately, this is becoming a popular way to raise awareness that we need more conversations about insurance coverage instead of media coverage. The sad truth is people will invest in gossip before they would an Insurance policy.

4. **The Government takeover**

   This is a very well kept secret. Financial assistance is available to help pay for some or all of the funeral or burial costs of a loved one or parent.

Some states and counties listed at http://www.funerals.org may offer direct financial aid for paying these bills and the various expenses that may be incurred from a funeral.

Non-profit advice and referrals for funerals

The Funeral Consumers Alliance is a nonprofit organization that provides families with resources and educational materials on funeral choices.

The agency does provide information on how to go about shopping and saving money. There is advice on everything from paying for items and services such as caskets, cemeteries, urns, funeral homes, or monuments. Or some clients may learn about how to get help in the form of free services, whether it is a funeral service, casket, or burial plot.

Services offered can easily save families more than $10,000 on their burial and funeral costs, and help reduce a lot of heartache that may arise for the family from overwhelming bills during a tremendously stressful time.
The non-profit Funeral Consumers Alliance partners with a number of affiliates that operate across the nation. If you need help, guidance, or advice, consider contacting the Funeral Consumer's Alliance for information. The staff will direct the client to the most effective resource for their needs.

Some of the non-profits as well as charities affiliated with Funeral Memorial Society of America provide education. In general, it is a good bet that by supporting and joining a local FCA organization that you will be able to save hundreds or even thousands of dollars on unnecessary funeral and burial costs. Savings may also be negotiated on caskets, cremation costs and other services.

An updated list of local organizations can be found at **funerals.org**. The main office of Funeral Consumers Alliance can be reached at 1-802-482-3437.

An alphabetical list of state, county government, and other non-profit help with funeral or burial costs, can be found at http://www.funerals.org.

Federal Government Assistance with Funerals

Help with funeral expenses from the federal government is limited, but there are some programs which may be able to help you.

Among these are:
Social Security (800-772-1213 / website)
The Veterans Administration (855-574-7286 / website)
The Federal Emergency Management Agency (FEMA) (800-621-3362 / website) National Center for Victims of Crime (202-467-8700 / website)

We have provided a list below of the benefits and resources that you should ask about at the federal government organizations.

Social Security Survivors Benefits

Social Security One-Time Death Benefit
You should notify the Social Security Administration as soon as possible after the death. If you are working with a funeral director, he or she may handle the notification for you, but you should confirm this since you must apply within two years of death. If you are taking care of notification, you must do so in person at a local social security office or by calling 1-800-772-1213. You cannot apply online.

Social Security Monthly Benefits
For complete information on eligibility, we recommend that you contact the Social Security Administration.

Eligible survivors include:
- A widow or widower age 60 or older (50 if disabled), or at any age if caring for an entitled child who is under 16 or disabled.
- A divorced widow or widower age 60 or older (50 if disabled) if the marriage lasted ten years, or if caring for an entitled child who is under

16 or disabled.
- Unmarried children under age 18 and age 19 if they are attending a primary or secondary school full-time; and under certain circumstances, benefits can be paid to stepchildren, grandchildren or adopted children.
- Children who were disabled before reaching 22, as long as they remained disabled. Dependent parent or parents 62 or older.

How to Apply

You cannot apply for Social Security benefits online. To apply, visit your local Social Security office or call 1-800-772-1213. You will need the following information when you apply:

- Death certificate.
- Social security numbers — the deceased, the applicant, dependent children. Applicant's birth certificate.
- Marriage certificate and divorce papers, as applicable.
- W-2 forms or federal self-employment tax return for deceased worker for the most recent year. Bank and account number for direct deposit of benefits.
- If you are already receiving benefits as a husband or wife on your spouse's record when she or he dies, immediately report the death to Social Security to have your payments changed to survivor benefits. If you are receiving benefits based on your work record, complete an application and Social Security will determine if you can receive more under survivor benefits.

For more information on applying for Social Security benefits visit: www.ssa.gov or call 1-800-772-1213.

Veterans Benefits for Funerals and Burials
Service-related Death

You should always check to make sure that you have the most current information before you decide your eligibility. Visit the VA Burial Benefits Eligibility Page.

You can apply for benefits online at https://www.vets.gov/burials-and-memorials/pre-need/. To apply by paper application you will need to complete VA Form 21P530, Application for Burial Allowance. For more information on how to complete the paper form you can visit the link above. Your local regional benefit office can also assist you.

CEMETERIES

The National Cemetery Scheduling Office is the organization that can help you make arrangements to have an eligible Service Member, Veteran, Spouse, or dependent buried in a national cemetery. A funeral director can help you make arrangements, or you can contact the office at 800-535-1117.

For information on burial at sea, contact the United States Navy Mortuary Affairs office toll-free at 1-888-647-6676, and select option 4. For more information on Veteran's benefits visit https://www.va.gov/ or call 1-855-574-7286. Disaster Relief FEMA provides some assistance with funeral expenses if you are in a Presidentially declared disaster area and the death is caused as a direct result of the disaster. The amount that you are eligible for is determined by the state, territory, or tribal government. You can reside outside the declared area but the death must be caused by the emergency.

To be eligible, the deceased must:

- Be a U.S. citizen, non-citizen national, or qualified alien. Must have a verifiable identity.
- Burial insurance or other forms of assistance must be insufficient to meet the disaster-caused needs.

- Required documentation must be provided. To see exactly what documentation is required visit the FEMA funeral assistance page.
- FEMA will only provide assistance for expenses directly related to funeral or burial. Items such as an obituary, flowers, or catering are not covered.

Because the number of awards and details of how to apply can vary depending on the disaster, we recommend that you contact FEMA (800) 621-3362) to discuss your specific circumstances.

Victim's Assistance

The National Center maintains a listing of the programs offered by each state. To find out what type of benefits your state offers click here. To contact the National Center, call (202) 467-8700.

Utilized Insurance Agents

Lance Bankers Life

101 Bullitt Lane, Suite 207

Louisville, KY 40222

7706088427

Cordell Blair

Prime American Insurance

4229 Bardstown Rd

Louisville, 40218

5025339442

Reflection

Living Witness

I am a Living Witness for the child under 18 years of age. After losing my son at age 18, I now feel every young person should have a living witness document to refer to if something were to happen to them.

- I felt like this was the hardest part about his Funeral the not knowing......
- What he wanted to wear
- Who he wanted to attend
- Who shouldn't attend
- Did he want to be an organ donor of any kind
- What music or song did he want to be played or poems read
- Resting Preference-Buried or cremated?
- Who does he / she want to have your belongings?
- I believe Creating A living memory video would be best.

Update it every 2 years until their 22nd birthday

I feel every parent will make the necessary arrangement but the peace of mind knowing you honored their last request would make a world of difference to your heart.

Have it signed personalized, notarized and kept with your insurance policy information.

Reflection

Self-Care is Like a Medicine to a Mourner

Self-care plays a big part in your overall healing process. There's no limit set on how much or how many **Self-Help Groups** you should join or the crafting projects you should start. Do yourself the favor of exploring different forms of self-care. For example:

- Nature is a great source of taking your mind on a healthy though Safari.
- Take naps you feel better if you get proper rest.
- Journal your thoughts and emotions you never know What could be birthed from your pain.
- Make an appointment to see your doctor for a check-up. Let them know that you are grieving the loss of your loved one. If you are struggling with depression, not sleeping properly or suffering with any form of anxiety, they can help you with a healthy plan of action.
- Go get your hair done, have someone give you a great shampoo & style it does a world of good.
- Music is a great time travel to experience.
- Reading will allow your mind to focus on a new novel.
- Go get a body Massage- they provide a great stress reliever and relaxation.
- Mediation is a way of activating self-reflection and clearing your personal Aura. I enjoy using aromatherapy scents.
- Coloring and doodling really helped me as well with stress relief. See page 113 for a free download of coloring sheets.

It's all up to you. The reality is that no two mourners are exactly alike, yet we are very similar to one another. Getting what you need provides you with the Grace and tolerance to support others in this season of sadness.

For more information and help with what your body is actually going through during the grieving process, visit this website: http://www.greekmedicine.net/hygiene/Emotions_and_Organs.html

Reflection

Planning the Funeral Arrangements

Funeral Planning Checklist

Funeral Program and Obituary

_____ Place of birth, death

_____ Parents

_____ Siblings

_____ School

_____ Work

_____ Church

_____ Spouse/Partner

_____ Children

_____ Nieces/Nephew

_____ Special Shouts

_____ Poem

_____ Music

_____ Minister

_____ Pallbearers

_____ Funeral Home

_____ Cemetery

_____ Repass/Church

_____ Funeral Home

Funeral Home Options

Hathaway and Clark

2718 Virginia Ave.

Louisville, KY 40211

(502) 778-7096

W.T. Shumake & Daughters

3815 Newburg Rd.

Louisville, KY 40218

(502) 458-6214

Newcomer Cremations, Funerals & Receptions, Southwest Louisville Chapel

10304 Dixie Hwy.

Louisville, KY 40272

502-935-0056

Cremation vs. Burial

For our beloved AJ we made the hard choice of having him cremated. We were the first on both sides of our family to choose this method. There were a lot of family members with mixed emotions and they couldn't believe that we wanted to destroy are perfectly assembled son.
The only thing they were considering was what we would do with his remains and who would inherit him if something were to happen to us.

We explained our views and reasons for choosing the way we did and for us, the pros out-weighed the cons and now others have followed our lead.

Our three main reason we cremated AJ were
1. We never wanted to be without him
2. We wanted to still celebrate with him physically.
3. We never wanted to miss visiting him due to bad weather or if we decided to move away.

Here are some facts I researched on the matter, Is it better to get buried or cremated?

The Major Differences

Let's begin by looking at some of the differences and distinctions between cremation and burial. When a body is cremated, it is incinerated so that all that remains are ashes. With a burial, the body remains intact. Both cremation and burial can take place immediately after death, following a traditional funeral service or before a memorial service. In the case of a burial, the body can be interred in the ground or entombed in a mausoleum. By comparison, cremated remains can be kept by the family, scattered, buried in the ground, or entombed in a columbarium. Of the two, cremation is generally the more economical choice.

Respect For The Remains

When we speak to people who are deciding between burial and cremation, some common themes and questions recur. One of the most common concerns people express is a desire to be respectful of the deceased's memory and by extension of their body. It's interesting to note, however that for some people, that means preserving the integrity of the body, while for others, the thought of allowing the remains to decay underground is simply unacceptable.

In many cultures and faiths, viewing the body is an important part of the funeral ritual. Many people mistakenly believe that choosing cremation as an option makes this impossible. In fact, it is not uncommon for a viewing to take place before cremation.

Impact on the Environment

If choosing an option that is environmentally friendly is important to you, then there are pros and cons for both burial and cremation. There is some debate among supporters of either choice as to which has the least negative impact on the environment. Some believe that a significant amount of pollutants is released during the cremation process, while others cite the lack of biodegradability of materials used in traditional caskets as well as the toxicity of embalming fluids as the reason why they feel cremation is a better green choice.

There has been a recent rise in popularity in what is commonly known as natural or eco-burials. These types of burials do not use embalming fluids and coffins are made of environmentally friendly and biodegradable materials.

Jan 29, 2016 Post Entry at: https://feeandsons.com

10 Important Cremation Vs Burial Pros & Cons You Should Consider
It's probably the biggest decision you're going to make when it comes to making funeral plans.

So, what's the better Burial or Cremation?

Well the truth is, there's no easy answer.

Both have their pro's and con's which we'll discuss in detail.

The decision will come down to what's right for you and your family.

And this will be based on your budget, personal beliefs, religion, and other factors.

If you're not sure yet, take your time to go through some of these important pro's and con's.

Cremation & Burial Statistics
There's no doubt that cremation is on the rise. According to the Cremation Association of North America (CANA), the rate has grown from 48.6 in (2015) and is expected to rise to 54.3 by(2020).

A recent study by Harris Poll, which was commissioned by the Funeral and Memorial Information Council (FAMIC,) reported that 65% of Americans were definitely or likely to choose being cremated.

These statistics indicate that at this time, the decision to be cremated versus buried is close to half and half, but appear to be leaning towards the latter in the future.

Burial Vs Cremation: Cost Comparison

Frequently, people choose cremation because they perceive it to be cheaper than burial.

Below is a breakdown of the approximate costs associated with each one, beginning with the basic costs and then with the added options that may be offered:

Basic Burial Services:

Fee for a basic service – $2000
Transportation of the body to the funeral home – $300
Preparation of the body – $200
Embalming – $700
Car for the transportation of flowers and other belongings – $130 Use of the staff and facility for the viewing and funeral – $900 Hearse – $300
Memorial print package such as memorial directories, registration book, acknowledgement cards – $150

Additional Burial Costs:

Grave plot- $1000 Burial vault – $1300
Opening and closing fee – $1200 Casket (metal) – $1000 – $15000 Headstone – $1500

Additional Cremation Costs: Casket rental – $1000

Urn – $250

Cremation – $30

Direct Cremation:
Here is a breakdown of what is included:

The body is cremated immediately after death. You will engage the services of a crematory, bypassing the expense of a funeral home.
The body can be cremated in a simple cardboard container. No memorial service is held.
No embalming or other preparations of the body are necessary because there is no service, viewing, or wake.

Dealing directly with a Crematorium

In most areas, you can transport the body to the crematorium and take care of the paperwork such as the death certificate and transit permits yourself.

In some states you will have to hire a funeral director for these services. Therefore, you should look into your state's requirements in advance.

The Cost of Direct Cremation

It can be as low as $700 and usually no higher than around $2000, depending on what is mandatory in your state and also with who you deal with.

Pro's & Cons of Cremation & Burial Benefits of Cremation:

- You can still have a funeral service and burial before or after
- It is less costly than burial, although many people are talked into spending more than anticipated.
- It's quicker. Making these decisions can be a difficult and time consuming ordeal, especially when doing so during your time of loss.
- It is frequently considered more environmentally friendly. Burial is a source of environmental contaminants including the casket.
- Takes up less land and helps with the problem of overcrowded cemeteries.

- It is portable, so the ashes can be transported. You can put the ashes in an urn or other container and take them with you if you move.
- Families have more time to decide what to do with the ashes after the body has been cremated. Ideas include scattering ashes, interment, cremation jewelry, cremation diamonds, and cremation art are just a few.

Disadvantages of Cremation:

- May be against the deceased's or a family member's religion.
- It's a permanent decision and cannot be exhumed at a later date. Sometimes makes it more difficult for loved ones to mourn.
- Should you want to know more, our how does cremation work guide goes through everything you need to know about the process.

Advantages of Burial:

- Provides a gravesite for family and friends to visit
- Considered a more natural method by some
- Required by some religions
- The body can be exhumed if necessary
- May give loved ones more closure

Disadvantages of Burial:

- Normally much more expensive than cremating
- Difficult for loved ones who live away to visit
- Cemeteries can have restrictions on leaving flowers, taking pictures, or visiting hours

Cremation Urn Costs

Double Companion Urn

If you're looking to save on costs, it might be worth purchasing the urn online. There's so many different types of urns and your choice will depend on a number of things.

Here are some types of urns to consider and ask about:

- Double Urns

- Cremation Boxes

- Stylish Wooden Cremation Box

- Biodegradable Urns

- Infant Urns

———————————————————-

What does the Bible say about Cremation?

Cremation in the Bible and references to burial are mentioned throughout the course of it. It was the usual practice by the ancient Greeks, but the Hebrews used burial. Both methods were used by the Romans.

Many feel that had God seen cremating as sinful, he would have condemned it as he did with other imprudent religious practices.

Does cremation interfere with the resurrection?

Some are afraid that resurrections will not be possible because the body is no longer whole, however, even with a conventional burial, the body eventually decomposes and the body no longer exists.

It may answer that question if you consider that firemen frequently burn to death in their line of duty. In some cultures, stillborn infants are immediately cremated.

The lack of their bodies would surely not deprive those individuals of the resurrection.

Ecclesiastes 12:7 - "Then the dust will return to the earth as it was and the spirit will return to God who gave it."

Religious perspectives on cremation

For a complete list of religions and their perspectives on Cremation as well as other information on cremation, visit:
https://cremationinstitute.com/cremation-vs-burial/

Premonition Intuition Dreams

Before, during, and after the loss of a loved one you may feel like you're losing your mind. Life sometimes sends you signs and clues that may not make sense or become your truth for many years. When you do put it all together, it will read like a good mystery book with your name all over it.

1.   premonition (plural premonitions) - A clairvoyant or clairaudient experience, such as a dream, which resonates with some event in the future.

Synonym: vision

A strong intuition that something is about to happen (usually something negative, but not exclusively).

Synonyms: bad feeling, gut feeling, foreboding, hunch, second sight (informal)

https://www.merriam-webster.com/dictionary/premonition

My Truth

I would often have this same dream and I didn't understand what the connection was. This was months before I knew the birth and sex know of my son AJ.

I kept having a continuous replay of this hospital room where a badly injured young man would always appear. I didn't recognize who this person was. I tried to see if he was a family member or a friend's face but I could never make out who that person was. However, I felt a connection to this human being and every time I had the dream I wanted to help this stranger. Well twenty-four years later I now know it was my future preparing me for the reality in which I now live. That strange person was my son that I hadn't even met yet. I still get goosebumps from this unveiling.

Intuition is the ability to acquire knowledge without recourse to conscious reasoning. Different writers give the word "intuition" a great variety of different meanings, ranging from direct access to unconscious knowledge, unconscious cognition, inner sensing, inner insight to unconscious pattern-recognition and the ability to understand something instinctively, without the need for conscious reasoning.

The word intuition comes from the Latin verb intueri translated as "consider" or from the late middle English word intuit, "to contemplate."

Philosophy

Several weeks before AJ's death I had this funny feeling that came out of the blue every time the local news channel came on the television. Literally, my heart would flutter. I still couldn't tell you why but I would feel anxious to do a quick roll call on my family to make sure everyone was safe and okay. They all would answer and my heart would be soothed with reassurance. But I understand now that I was mentally being conditioned to cope with my truth.

The sound of the news coming on would soon be the warning sign broadcasting to the world our son's face all over it. And the repeat announcement would serve as proof my roll call has an absent member, our beloved son AJ.

A dream is a succession of images, ideas, emotions, and sensations that usually occur involuntarily in the mind during certain stages of sleep. The content and purpose of dreams are not fully understood, although they have been a topic of scientific, philosophical and religious interest throughout recorded history.

After we found out AJ had died, I didn't rest at all that first night. I believe I cried and prayed for a full twenty-four hours. I remember becoming so exhausted I just passed out fully dressed across my bed. I was out cold, as my husband explained to me. He didn't bother me because he knew I needed the rest.

I felt extremely sad and missed my son so much. I just kept saying how desperately I wanted to see him again. Well that night I experienced a real-life encounter with my child. I physically felt him hug me, kiss my face and just repeat to me I love you mama. I never saw his face but I felt his hand that embraced me and his full lips that kissed my cheek. But the moment I went to reach out to him and give back that same loving embrace I woke from my slumber only to be left alone. He wasn't in my room. I had dreamt of this visit.

The dream didn't last long enough for my heart. To this day, no one can make me believe otherwise that this wasn't a real visit because my heart felt his. If only I could have just loved him back to life. That would have been one sweet dream.

After my visitation with AJ, I began to research this experience to make sure this was even something logical that had happened before to other mourners, and not just me hallucinating from being sleep deprived. I needed to have the facts so that I didn't drive myself crazy or have others thinking I was.

Characteristics of Visitation Dreams

Deceased loved ones who have crossed to the Light can and do visit us in our dreams. These types of dreams are often referred to as "visitation dreams," and they can provide us with great comfort. Why do deceased loved ones come to us in our dreams? It is actually easier for spiritual entities of all kinds (e.g., deceased loved ones, guides, angels) to communicate with us while we are sleeping. Why? Because when sleeping, we are in that "in between place" between our earthly reality and "the other side of the veil" (the spiritual world). During this time, our rational mind and our ego are not engaged. Things can happen in our dream world that we would normally stop or discount while awake.

For example, when someone who has died comes to visit us in our dreams, we aren't as likely to have the "rational thought" that this person is actually dead and shouldn't be in our dream. When they appear, we accept that person's presence without argument.

Is every dream a visitation dream? Although I would love to say that you are having a visitation dream every time your beloved Grandfather Lou appears in a dream, but this is not the case. Why? Here is how most of our "everyday dreams" are created. Think of your dream as a play or a movie. Your subconscious mind is the director that must select who will play the different roles. For example, that role might need someone who is a businessman, so your beloved grandfather Lou is selected because he was a successful businessman. Or perhaps the role requires a loving mother figure; then perhaps your mother Betty is chosen because she was a very loving presence in your life when you were a child.

Based on all the people you have known during your lifetime (even those you may not consciously remember and possibly even people from past lives), the director selects the best actor for that part. Sometimes the actor who is selected is alive; sometimes the actor has passed. But the actor is simply "the best person for the job" because he or she fits the requirements you need for that dream.

8 Characteristics of True Visitation Dreams

True "visitation dreams" are actually very easy to identify because they are very different than "everyday dreams." Characteristics of most (but not all) visitation dreams include the following:

Characteristic #1: The most important characteristic of a true visitation dream is that it feels "real." It will also be very vivid.

Characteristic #2: If you have to ask whether the visitation dream was really a visitation dream, then it probably was NOT a visitation dream. They are so real and vivid that you won't have to ask this question. When you do have a visitation dream, you may wonder if it was truly real; but in your heart or gut, you will "know" it was real.

Characteristic #3: Because they are so real and so vivid, you will remember visitation dreams very clearly for days, months, years . . . probably for your entire lifetime!

Characteristic #4: The person (or animal) will almost always appear in the dream to be completely healthy and behaving in a loving manner. They will rarely appear sick or injured. They will never be angry, disappointed, depressed, or punishing. They will be "whole, complete, and perfect" because they are now reconnected with God/Source energy.

Characteristic #5: Whether or not they speak to you verbally in the dream, they will communicate very clearly. (NOTE: As you'll see in the next two examples, in neither of the dreams did actual verbal communication occur; the messages were conveyed telepathically and were completely clear.)

Characteristic #6: When they do communicate (either verbally or non-verbally), it isn't because they want to engage in idle "chit-chat." It isn't easy for deceased loved ones to enter a dream. They come with a purpose, and they will convey the message and then be gone.

Characteristic #7: Most often, their messages fall into the category of "reassurance." They come to let you know that they are fine and that they want you to be happy. Occasionally, they will come with a warning; however, when giving a warning, they will give you loving support and you will feel reassured by their presence.

Characteristic #8: After a visitation dream, when you wake up, you will often be filled with a sense of peace and love.

https://annereith.com/8-characteristics-of-visitation-dreams/

Some people will choose to dismiss the signs as if they are, coincidence or just incidentals. I'm not telling you to believe either way that is your choice, but remember we all are spiritual beings having a human experience. when we return to the spirit that is who return to visit you.

Reflection

WHO IS A GRIEVING MOTHER?

Does she look different from one who is not?
Is her pain visible in the smile she sometimes forces... behind the eyes on the verge of tears?
Can you see the aging her body feels from the trauma of loss? She's one who still pictures herself from before the loss...
and is sometimes caught off guard at the reflection looking back from the mirror. Who is a grieving mother?
She's one who ignores a baby shower or birthday invitation one day, because the pain is still too raw.
And the next, celebrates the small milestones, for she knows how precious they are.
She's one who boxes up a lifetime of memories in an afternoon to spare others the pain. Yet years later still can't dredge up the courage to go through them again.
Who is a grieving mother?
She's one who holds it together in the big things and falls apart over spilled milk.
Who loves deeply those closest to her, but keeps her heart guarded for protection from others? She's one who grimaces at the first laughs after loss, but later laughs louder than most.
Who finds joy in the simple things and relishes every day moments? Who is a grieving mother?
She's one held hostage by dates on the calendar and unexpected triggers.
And one who will always pause for sunsets, butterflies, and sweet signs from above. She's one who let's go of friends unable to support her.
And one who treasures those who didn't walk away. Who is a grieving mother?
She's one who can experience an array of emotions on any given day. And one who wishes tears would come when numbness covers her.
She's one who screams at God one moment and clings to him the next.
Who didn't expect her faith to grow so much from the most important

unanswered prayer she ever spoke?
Who is a grieving mother?
She is one as complicated as the grief she carries. "Do not judge the Grieving Mother.
She comes in many forms.
She is breathing, but she is dying.
She may look young, but inside she has become ancient. She smiles, but her heart sobs.
She walks, she talks, she cooks, she cleans, she works, she IS but she IS NOT, all at once.
She is here, but part of her is elsewhere for eternity."

~ Author Unknown ~

I live for us both Now.......

The hole I have in my heart is now a portal for my memories time has no expiration you & I will always meet here.

You often come back and visit my thoughts right when I need you. AJ, you've been a mama's boy since birth. I never wanted to close you out of my life.

Just because you're no longer here physically on earth, that doesn't mean a thing to me.

I loved you before I ever met you so you know I can't ever forget you; that would be insane. I have loved you from the day you were born on 3/14/96 until

2/7/15, which is the day you took your last breath  .

Even when it hurts, I'll bear with the pain. From (labor to loss)you've always been worth it. You're priceless to Me.

Baby boy, this love we share is for infinity.

Death, you have no power over my love for my child he's mine forever.

We share umbilical cord love .

Reflection

Top 10 Things You Should Never Say to a Mourning Mother!

But because it's been asked I'll answer it one last time for All the mourning mother's across the world.

- (You'll be ok) no , I'm not OK I'm sure I want be for a while.
- (You're so Strong) I don't feel strong I feel weak and vulnerable right now .
- (You can have another child) having another child wouldn't replace the child I've lost .
- (They're in a better place) what better place could your child be then with its mother & love ones.
- (Let the dead Bury the dead) if I hear that one more time I'll scream like your killing Me.
- No one wants to hear that even if's biblically the truth .
- (You're still mourning Get over it) yes I'm still mourning over my child that I lost that I will Never get to hear or see touch or live this LIFE with again !
- (How are you doing)do you really want an answer to this obvious question my mind couldn't even begin to Dissect - the reason someone would ask a grieving mother this expecting her to even form you up an example of the pain she's experiencing ,so don't ask because I couldn't begin tell you how I'm doing.
- (I can only imagine how you feeling) what I can't believe is that you would try to imagine this pain this heartache & mental headache you want to imagine this using your child as an example wow please don't manifest something like that it's not for you to ever imagine.
- (I don't know how your holding up) it's by the grace of God each and every day comes with a new set of mind mazes & triggers but my faith is what guides me through
- (At least you can say you had a child) at least wow you're right but the point to highlight is the loss as a mourning mother we want you to recognize and remember we lost a child

Our life's daily routine is totally off course. The way we identify ourselves has been altered. Our mindset & Priority's had been hacked. The sense of time is senseless. Time doesn't matter anymore as mourning mothers, we stopped counting at the casket!

We want get to count on planning
- Birthday parties
- School pictures
- Field trips
- Family vacations
- Proms
- Graduation
- First job
- College
- Engagements
- wedding
- Grandchildren
- Them being with us on the holidays
- OR when we'll need them most in our old age.

The list was Just to give you an idea of what we had to look forward to. It was never designed for a mother to bury her child and the fact that this is our truth. Please stop counting on us to be who you once knew, that person died with our child.

Support a mourning mother by taking a moment to Pause & stop counting and recognize & realize that we lost a part of us that made (us). The reality is we will never get to be that person again for Nobody!

From a mourning mother's heart, please don't tell us how to feel. The reality is this is a very personal subject! All we ask is that you respect our space & truth.

We lost our child.

MY GRIEF RIGHTS

BY DR. ALAN D. WOLFELT

Someone you love has died. You are probably having many hurtful and scary thoughts and feelings right now. Those thoughts and feelings are called grief. Grief is a normal (though really hard) thing everyone goes through after someone they love has died.

These 10 rights will help you understand your grief and, over time, feel better about life again. Hang this poster somewhere you'll see it often. Re-reading it will help keep you on track as you move through your grief. You can also ask the grown-ups in your life to read the list so they'll remember to help you in the best ways they can.

1. I have the right to have my own feelings about the death. I might feel mad, sad, or lonely. I might feel scared or relieved. I might feel numb or sometimes not anything at all. No one will feel exactly like I do.

2. I have the right to talk about my grief whenever I feel like it. When I need to talk, I will find someone who will listen to me and love me. When I don't want to talk about it, that's OK, too.

3. I have the right to show my feelings of grief in my own way. Other grieving kids like to play as they'll feel better for a while. I can play or laugh, too. I might also get mad and do angry things. That doesn't mean I'm bad, it just means I have scary feelings that I need help with.

4. I have the right to need other people to help me with my grief, especially grown-ups who care about me. Mostly I need them to pay attention to what I'm feeling and saying and to love me no matter what.

5. I have the right to get upset about little things. I might feel grumpy and have trouble getting along with others sometimes.

6. I have the right to have "griefbursts." Griefbursts are sudden feelings of sadness that just hit me sometimes—even a long time after the death. Griefbursts can be really strong and even scary. When they happen, I might need to ask someone for help.

7. I have the right to use my beliefs about God to help me with my feelings of grief. Praying might make me feel better and somehow closer to the person who died.

8. I have the right to try to understand why the person I love died. But it's OK if I don't find an answer. "Why?" questions about life and death are the hardest questions in the world.

9. I have the right to remember the person who died. I can also talk about my memories. Sometimes those memories will be happy, and sometimes they might be sad. Either way, remembering helps me.

10. I have the right to grieve and, over time, to heal. I'll go on to live a happy life, and the life and death of the person I miss will always be a part of me.

https://www.centerforloss.com/bookstore/my-grief-rights-poster/

Reflection

Caution I'm Fragile and Mending from Mourning.....

As a mourning parent, Self-Care is very important. You need to get Plenty of sleep.

Why? Studies show sleep reboots the Immune system. Rest also provides an unconscious way of temporarily escaping the grips of Grief. You'll need your strength to make it through another day.

Take time for yourself at least 45 minutes to an hour a day just for you. This time is set around the same time every day to set order and train those around you to respect this time & space.

Assign tasks to people that have asked how they can help support you through this time of grief.

If you have other children, allow them to help you do chores. They want to help see you through this as well.

If you have multiple children, take a day to share and support each child individually. They need this nurturing time to share with you their personal feelings that they might not want their other siblings to know about as they feel grief.

Handling Friends & Family

- Let your No ! mean No ! and your yes be just that .
- Teach people how to handle your fragileness from mourning . Your emotions can seem to be unstable
- like symptoms of a bipolar disorder. And that normal
- Your senses or off and you could feel fine one hour and totally overwhelmed in the next breath.
- Go on daily Nature Walks , get plenty of fresh air , drink plenty of water to stay hydrated.
- Take supplements to stay balanced.
- If possible, get a babysitter for the other children.
- Find a day spa or go on a mini getaway, or even find a local healing retreat session to attend for support.

Most importantly…….

- Don't agree to over exerting yourself to please others' requests of you.
- If you've been asked to do more than you're willing to spare yourself to do, don't do it.
- If going to that baby shower is too much don't Go
- If Going to the party is too much don't Go
- If going to the wedding is too much don't Go
- If going to another funeral is too much Don't Go
- If allowing the company of family & friends coming over & staying for long periods of time becomes too much, don't do it .

- Set visiting hours like the hospital after all you are trying to heal and rest.

You have to do what is best for your healing process. Just Send a card or a gift and save your energy. In the end, if you aren't okay and feel uncomfortable with being in large crowds, don't go. Your family or friends should understand and expect your gift or card as a form of being grateful for the invite. If talking about your child with someone you don't want to share with comes up, feel free to safeguard your heart by politely changing the subject or excusing yourself from the conversation.

Reflection

Being Married and Mourning

This has been the hardest balancing act. I say "act" because we are life partners that took vows; for better or worse, through sickness and in health, until death parts us. Not the death of losing our child that the two of made together out of this loving union.

The fact that we try to be strong for one another sometimes feels overwhelming, overbearing and overall, just too much at times. When you're married you share everything together but when it comes to pain, we try to hold onto it separately, feeling as if we are doing it out of love for the other spouse. When in fact, thinking for one another is the worst thing to do as a grieving couple.

The loss of your child can't be handled like a monthly budget, a planned vacation, or a family meeting. If one of you doesn't participate it, is business as usual. That's not how mourning works. The two of you are now collectively and personally experiencing the loss of your child, the two experiences are the same but totally different.

How do you ask? The mother has the umbilical cord that is a unifying connection to the child. Her love for the child starts at the positive pregnancy test and confirmed when she heard the unborn child's heartbeat. This is solidified from the first kick she felt when no one else could feel what she felt. While the father has the bond of love with the child, there is a difference. What's the difference you ask? It's Space and time. The child shared a space in the mother's womb, while the father waited patiently for the baton to be passed, so that he too could start his journey to experience the bonding of unconditional love.

Ultimately the child can, and even may have favored one parent over the other. However, in a loving nurturing family, the child had the support of both parents.

Parent A will be labeled as the (need parent)

Parent B will be labeled as the (want parent).

Only the child knows who parent A & B are in their life.

As we grew in love with this child, they were studying us while we were loving them. So yes, I'm sure the child used this to their advantage as soon as they knew they had those superpowers. Manipulation is very common when you're focused on being the best parent possible to your child.

Remember, before marriage you two were individuals that were parented by 4 other individuals. Depending on each person's parenting style, this new grandchild may have entered into the family that already had set ways. Generations of traditions and memories that reminiscent of how we all were raised. So, for better or worse, we had an idea of how we wanted our child to be raised and we decided to use both of our blended upbringings.

This is the gray area for even healthy marriages. Now add in death, grief and blame. After a loss of a child, the "what if's", the "if you would have", and "it's your fault", come flying out of thin air.

Your mind will take you through a maze, it will have you traveling down memory lane but in the wrong direction. You'll find yourself arguing about how you both handled disciplining & caring for the deceased child. Why is that you ask? Because you both have a need to place your pain somewhere. The fact is, the closest person to you, gets the worst part of the remorseful backlash. The old saying is true, "Hurt people – Hurt people", and even the most loving couple will fall prey to the evil plot.

As a married and mourning mother, I need you to hear me clearly when I say, your child's death is not your fault if you had nothing to do with how they died. Take yourself off the jury and understand your parenting is not on trial. So, stop adding Guilt to your Grief. However, you may need a mediator in your case. This person is better known as a marriage counselor and make sure that this person specializes in grief.

Honestly, we can't fight with the truth and fighting with each other will cause another loss resulting in the destruction of the foundation.

So please, get some reinforcement. You two can make it through this and heal together, with help and hope.

Sincerely,

The Smiths

Reflection

An Advocating Voice for the Child(ren) Left Behind, with the Mourning Parent(s).

A child raised in a traditional or co-parent environment is raised with a certain level of respect, order and rules. This creates the family's circle of trust and acceptable behaviors. This understanding is taught an early age and it follows the child throughout their life.

I can hear the list of clichés even now as I write. As they were once rehearsed to me, I have repeated them to my own children.

"What goes on in this house, stays in this house."
"Don't talk to strangers", (especially about your family's business).
"Keep your opinions to yourself."
"Don't you Dare, tell me- the adult what to do."
"Stay in a child's place."
"You have to pay the cost, to be the boss."
"This is my house, my rules."
"If you don't like it here, then when you are old enough, you can leave."
"Do as I say, not as I do."
"Stay out of grown folks' business."

Now, apply all of these rules to the child muted in emotional silence and pain. This creates conflict between grief and what they have been taught their entire life.

Each day, they live with the reality of what grief and loss looks like from their young lens. they began to build a wall of remorse, resentment, regrets, rebellion and retaliation.

They may appear as just sad or the parent dismisses it as normal. This is easier for the parent to understand than doing a detailed debrief. It is more likely disturbing, when the child actually acts out or is labeled as, "not being their normal self."

This is where the unfair advantage of being an adult comes into play.

The parent may question the child regarding their behaviors. The parent's desire may be less about problem-solving and more so to get the problem solved!

Even the most respectful and well behaved child will have a breaking point. This will often be followed by a break-down.

They will begin to realize that this is not working and they can't continue life under the old protocol.

They really need your help to fix the brokenness they feel, but can't express because of your firm policies and procedures.

Understand this could be a form of breaching your love and loyalty contract.

The fear of losing their job of being a good child in your eyes is too much for them to process and handle under these conditions.

If they were allowed to answer you regarding their behavior, it wouldn't be the full version of the truth.

Why do you ask? They have watched you cry and mourn the loss of their sibling. In their own pain, they don't want to add to the sad space you've been in.

They may say the total opposite of their truth to keep the peace for as long as they can.

This is a very dangerous game of swim or drown. It is only but so long a person holding their breath under water has before they need to come up for air.

Often, when you see a person struggling to get to the top of the water for oxygen, they're fighting to survive and they really need help.

A lifeguard or someone near may need to administer mouth to mouth resuscitation to breathe life back into them.

Clearing their clogged airway of grief and guilt.

It's not always true that you're the one and only person who can save them.

Professional or appointed people can help save their life. If you're open to being rescued, they can teach you how to help with future swimming and C.P.R. (Child-Parent-Relationship) lessons.

Please allow your child the time and space until they're ready to voice their feelings with you or a professional.

The entire family is experiencing the loss of the same person who played a different role in everyone's life.

Yes mom, yes dad, you lost a child and you know exactly what that feels like. Imagine how difficult it must be, being a sibling to the deceased child.

They lost a buddy from birth, they share you, mom and you, dad with each other. They were friends and partners-in-crime too. They did life together and now that they're gone, they're lonely and left behind with you.

You are the closest person to them who can relate to their loss but, they can't tell you how they feel.

It is not because they don't love you, they just aren't sure how much more you can take. Please notice, if and when they leave the room when you're talking about their sibling. Notice when they start sleeping too much or missing meals.
Notice when they start getting in trouble at school, especially if they haven't done that before. Notice if they snap back within their conversations with you

and it seems disrespectful.

Notice if they gain or lose weight. Notice any new scars or injuries.

Notice if they are keeping new or different company. Notice if they start staying away from home.

Most importantly, notice and remember you're not the only one hurting. You are still the parent and have to tend to the living child(ren) who are still under your supervision and care.

Try your best to be the gentle giant, the superhero, the Pink Panther and detective-parent they need you to be.

One day, they will thank you for your love ❤ and support.

Celebrating the Holidays

https://www.nhpco.org

For many people, the holiday season is a special time of year marked by celebrations and gatherings with family and friends. For those struggling with the death of a loved one, the holidays may be a difficult time full of painful reminders that emphasize their sense of loss.

Often, friends and family members of those affected by a loss are unsure how to act or what to say to support their grieving loved one during the holidays.

National Hospice and Palliative Care Organization offers some suggestions for helping people deal with grief at this time of the year:

1.　Be supportive of the way the person chooses to handle the holidays. Some may wish to follow traditions; others may choose to avoid customs of the past and do something new. It's okay to do things differently.

2.　Offer to help the person with decorating or holiday baking. Both tasks can be overwhelming for someone who is grieving.

3.　Offer to help with holiday shopping. Share catalogs or online shopping sites that may be helpful.

4.　Invite the person to join you or your family during the holidays. You might invite them to join you for a religious service or at a holiday meal where they are a guest.

5.　Ask the person if he or she is interested in volunteering with you during the holidays. Doing something for someone else, such as helping at a soup kitchen or working with children, may help your loved one feel better about the holidays.

6.　Donate a gift or money in memory of the person's loved one. Remind the person that his or her loved one is not forgotten.

7.　Never tell someone that he or she should be "over it." Instead, give the person hope that, eventually, he or she will enjoy the holidays again.

8.	Be willing to listen. Active listening from friends and family is an important step to helping some cope with grief and heal.

9.	Remind the person that you are thinking of him or her and the loved one who died. Cards, phone calls and visits are great ways to stay in touch.

10.	Follow up after the holidays to check in. Given the activity of the season, some people may make it through the holidays without any issues but they might find the post-holiday period to be more difficult. So, checking in after the holidays to see how he or she may be doing is helpful.

In general, the best way to help those who are grieving during the holidays is to let them know you care and that their loved one is not forgotten.

Let Me Feed Your Broken Heart With Some Soul Food

Grandma's Southern Fried Chicken

You'll need

- 2 tablespoons paprika
- 2 tablespoons freshly ground black pepper
- 2 teaspoons garlic powder
- 2 teaspoons dried oregano
- 1/2 teaspoon cayenne pepper
- 2 teaspoons of onion powder
- 1 cup buttermilk
- 1 large egg
- Kosher salt
- One whole chicken, about 4 pounds, cut into 10 pieces or 3 1/2 pounds bone-in, skin-on breasts, legs, drumsticks, and/or wings
- 1 1/2 cups all-purpose flour
- 1/2 cup cornstarch
- 1 teaspoon baking powder
- 4 cups vegetable shortening or peanut oil

Ok are you ready …..here we Go

Directions

1.Combine the paprika, black pepper, garlic powder, oregano, and cayenne & onion powder in a small bowl and mix thoroughly with a fork.
2.
Whisk the buttermilk, egg, 1 tablespoon salt, and 2 tablespoons of the spice mixture in a large bowl. Add the chicken pieces and toss and turn to coat. Transfer the contents of the bowl to a gallon-sized zipper-lock freezer bag and refrigerate for at least 4 hours, and up to overnight, flipping the bag occasionally to redistribute the contents and coat the chicken evenly.

3. Whisk together the flour, cornstarch, baking powder, 2 teaspoons salt, and the remaining spice mixture in a large bowl. Add tablespoons of the marinade from the zipper-lock bag and work it into the flour with your fingertips. Remove one piece of chicken from the bag, at a time
Then place your chicken into the flour mixture, and toss to coat.

Continue adding chicken pieces to the flour mixture one at a time until they are all in the bowl.
Toss the chicken until every piece is thoroughly coated

4. Adjust an oven rack to the middle position and preheat the oven to 350°F. Heat the shortening or oil to 425°F in a 12-inch straight-sided cast-iron chicken fryer over medium-high heat. You may need to occasionally Adjust the heat as necessary to maintain the temperature, being careful not to let the oil get to hot.

5. Again start with One piece at a time, transfer the coated chicken to a fine-mesh strainer and shake to remove excess flour. Transfer to a wire rack set on a rimmed baking sheet. Once all the chicken pieces are coated, start placing your chicken in the oil skin side down in the pan.

The temperature should drop to 300°F; adjust the heat to maintain the temperature at 300°F for the duration of the cooking. Fry the chicken until it's a deep golden brown on the first side, about 6 minutes; do not move the chicken or start checking for doneness until it has fried for at least 3 minutes, or you may knock off the coating. Care- fully Now

flip the chicken pieces with tongs and cook until the second side is golden brown, about 3-4 minutes longer.
6. Transfer the chicken out of the oil onto a clean wire rack set on a rimmed baking sheet and place in the oven. Cook until an instant-read thermometer inserted into the thickest part of the breast registers 150°F and the legs register 165°F, 5 to 10 minutes; remove the chicken pieces to a paper-towel-lined plate as they reach their final temperature. Season with salt and serve.

Food fact- the Cooks always get left with the crumbs!

Gina's Good old fashioned Fresh Collard Greens mixed with Fresh Cabbage

You'll need 4 bundles of fresh collard greens & ahead of chopped cabbage

Before we go any further we need to soak and clean those greens & cabbage

Fill up the sink with cool water and white **vinegar** to cover the leaves

You should have about 1 part white **vinegar** to 3 parts water.

Let the **mixed greens soak** for about 10 minutes.

drain water and then rinse twice more without vinegar in the cool water again

Now lay out the leaf to remove the stems from the leaf Of all the greens roll leaf 2 or 3 times and chop for bite size pieces
Cabbage should be cut in half and then sliced or cut into small pieces
To comment the collard greens

Now you'll need 1 large yellow onion chopped
3 fresh garlic cloves chopped
Salt garlic powder accent onion powder 4 tablespoon of chicken bouillon powder
Franks hot sauce is optional
3 tablespoons of white sugar
I personal mix
1 cup full of white vinegar &
1 cup of apple cider vinegar
(or Optional)-use 2 Cups full of the same vinegar your choice
One red pepper chopper or a pinch of red peppers flakes for spice Optional
Some form of smoked meat I use one of the three
Smoked turkey butt ,smoked turkey legs or wings your choice
Chicken broth

In a stock pot began to add your smoked turkey meat
To a half filled pot of water

Let the smoked meat cook for
10 minutes to a rolling boil
remove from heat drain pot
refill your pot half way with the chicken broth & watered
this time re add the smoked meat and all your seasoning &
Your veggies-
(this part is optional)
I love adding in bacon grease to really lock it my seasoning
If not continue by
letting your mixer simmer for an hour then add your greens and cabbage allow them to slow cook for 1-1/2 hours
-Enjoy-

*Bonus side)-serve a nice refreshing Cucumber, Onion, and Tomato Salad

You'll need
1 cup water
1/2 cup distilled white vinegar

- 1/4 cup vegetable oil
- 1/4 cup sugar
- 2 teaspoons salt
- 1 tablespoon fresh, coarsely ground black pepper
- 1 table spoon of Italian seasoning
- 3 cucumbers, peeled and sliced 1/4-inch thick
- 3 tomatoes, cut into wedges
- 1 onion, sliced and separated into rings

- Prep15 minutes Ready In 2 h 15 m
- Whisk water, vinegar, oil, sugar, salt, and pepper & Italian seasoning together in a large bowl until smooth; add cucumbers, tomatoes, and onion and stir to coat.
- Cover bowl with plastic wrap; refrigerate at least 2 hours. Serve chilled next to your perfectly seasoned greens

Jeanine's Smack Ya Mama Mac & Cheese-

Ingredients

- 2 stick of unsalted butter
- 3 tablespoons all-purpose flour
- 2 1/2 cups half-and-half or whole milk or you can even use condensed milk it's totally optional (we mix all of them
- in our Mac & cheese -1 cp -half -and -half /1cp whole milk and 1/2 cup condensed milk
- 1 pound sharp Cheddar cheese the brand is optional
- 1/2 pound Colby cheese, brand optional
- 2 cups of Velveeta cheese
- 1 tablespoon Dijon mustard (optional)
- Pinch of nutmeg seasoning(optional)
- Pinch of cayenne pepper
- Pinch of white pepper
- Teaspoon of Salt
- 1 pound elbow
- macaroni 3/4 cup plain dry bread crumbs or 6 Pieces of white bread cut into small pieces

How to Make It

Step 1

Preheat the oven to 350°. Generously butter a shallow 2-quart baking dish. Melt 3 tablespoons of the butter in a large saucepan. Add the flour and cook over moderate heat for 2 minutes, stirring constantly. Add the half-and-half or your milk choice in cook over moderate heat, whisking constantly until thickened, about 3 minutes. Now Add one-half of the Cheddar and Colby cheeses and cook over low heat, stirring, until melted. Stir in the mustard, nutmeg and cayenne; season with salt and white pepper.

Step 2

Meanwhile, cook the elbow macaroni in a large pot of boiling salted water until al dente. (Soft not mushy)

Drain very well.
Return the macaroni to the pot. Add the cheese sauce and the remaining cheeses and stir until combined. Spread the macaroni in the prepared baking dish.

Step 3

In a small glass bowl, melt the remaining butter in a microwave oven.
Add the bread crumbs, or your small white bread pieces ,season with salt and pepper and stir until evenly moistened with the melted butter
Sprinkle the buttered bread crumbs over the macaroni and bake for 45 minutes, or until bubbling and golden on top. Let stand for 15 minutes before serving.

Active Time
45 MIN
Total Time
1 HR 30 MIN
Yield Serves : 6 to 8 servings
——————————————

Yummy Yams

INGREDIENTS

1/2 c. dark brown sugar
1/2 c. orange juice
3 tbsp. butter, plus more for pan
1 teaspoon of cinnamon
2 tbsp. bourbon (optional)
Pinch nutmeg
Pinch kosher salt
5 medium sweet potatoes (about 3 lb.)

1/4 cup of pecans optional

DIRECTIONS

- Preheat oven to 400°. Butter a medium baking dish.
- In a medium sauce pan over medium heat, combine sugar, orange juice, butter, cinnamon bourbon) if using, nutmeg, and salt. Stir to combine and bring to a boil, then reduce to a simmer and cook until it has thickened slightly, about 10 minutes

Meanwhile, prep potatoes:
Peel potatoes and slice into 1/2" rounds, then layer in prepared baking dish. Pour thickened syrup over potatoes and cover dish with aluminum foil.

- Bake 30 minutes, then remove foil add in chopped pecans and bake about 50 minutes to 1 hour more, basting with sauce every 15 minutes.
- Let cool slightly serving.

Dad's Deserve Dessert Tony's favorite - quick & easy low carb nutty buddy Peanut butter cookies

What you will need

- large egg
- Splenda; 1 cup – or your favorite (sugar) or a substitute
- 1 tsp. baking powder
- 1/2 tsp. vanilla
- 1 cup creamy or crunchy peanut butter
- 2. Tbs. of chopped pecans (optional)
- 1 tsp. water

INSTRUCTIONS:

1. Preheat the oven to 350 degrees.
2. In a mixing bowl, beat together the egg, (sugar)or substitute, baking powder and vanilla for about a minute.
3. Add the peanut butter and (Pecans optional)
4. water and beat together.
5. The mixture will be pretty dry; just make sure the peanut butter is blended in with the other ingredients.
6. Measure out a heaping teaspoon of batter for each cookie use a tablespoon then place on a baking tray that has been sprayed with non-stick cooking spray or lined with parchment paper.
7. Then using a fork, make indentations into each cookie. Spray the fork with cooking spray so it doesn't stick to the cookie.
8. Bake 12 – 15 minutes until cookies feel firm and are slightly browned.
9. Transfer the cookies to a baking rack and cool

(Try not to eat them all at once)

Danielle's Favorite Strawberry Lemonade

3 Fresh Lemon
3 Sliced Strawberry
Soda Water

In a gallon pitcher combine 1 cup lemon juice, 2 cup sugar, and 6 cups hot water. Stir. Adjust water to taste. add in
3oz of Island Oasis Strawberry Mix **now put chopped strawberries and lemons in your gallon pitcher and then add
a mint clove optional
Ice cubes
Serve**
————————-

(Adults only)
If you want to you can add 2oz of the vodka to make it a cocktail.

Nyias Favorite Banana Nut Bread

INGREDIENTS

- Cooking spray
- 8 tablespoons (1 stick) unsalted butter
- 1 cup granulated sugar
- 2 large eggs
- 1/4 cup milk
- 1 teaspoon vanilla extract
- 3 medium bananas, very ripe
- 2 cups all-purpose flour
- 1 teaspoon baking soda
- 1/4 teaspoon salt
- 1/2 cup chopped nuts
- we love pecans

Cooking EQUIPMENT

- 1 8x5-inch loaf pan
- Parchment paper
- Large bowl
- Whisk or fork, if making by hand
- Stand mixer or hand mixer, if not making by hand
- Spatula

INSTRUCTIONS

- **Heat the oven to 350°F and prep the pan.** Arrange a rack in the bottom third of the oven and heat to 350°F. Line an 8x5-inch loaf pan with parchment paper, letting the excess hang over the long sides to form a sling. Spray the inside with cooking spray. → *If using nuts, toast them in the oven for 10 minutes as the oven is pre-heating.*
- **Melt the butter.**
- Melt the butter in the microwave or over low heat on the stovetop. → *Alternatively, for a more cake-like banana bread, soften the butter (but do not melt) and cream it with the sugar in a stand mixer in the next step.*

- **Combine the butter and sugar.** Place the melted butter and sugar in a large bowl and whisk until combined. (Or cream the softened butter and sugar in a mixer until fluffy.)
- **Add the eggs.** Crack the eggs into the bowl. Whisk until completely combined and the mixture is smooth.
- **Add the milk and vanilla.** Whisk the milk and vanilla into the batter.
- **Mash in the bananas.** Peel the bananas and add them to the bowl. Using the end of the whisk or a dinner fork, mash them into the batter. Leave the bananas as chunky or as smooth as you prefer. If you prefer an entirely smooth banana bread, mash the bananas separately until no more lumps remain, and then whisk them into the batter.
- **Add the flour, baking soda, and salt.** Measure the flour, baking soda, and salt into the bowl. Switch to using a spatula and gently stir until the ingredients are *just* barely combined and no more dry flour is visible.
- **Fold in the nuts or chocolate, if using.** Last but not least, scatter the nuts or chocolate over the batter and gently fold them in.
- **Pour the batter into the pan.** Pour the batter into the prepared loaf pan, using the spatula to scrape all the batter from the bowl. Smooth the top of the batter.
- **Bake for 50 to 65 minutes.** Bake until the top of the cake is caramelized dark brown with some yellow interior peeking through and a toothpick or cake tester inserted into the middle comes out clean, 50 to 65 minutes. Baking time will vary slightly depending on the moisture and sugar content of your bananas — start checking around 50 minutes and then every 5 minutes after.
- **Cool in the pan for 10 minutes.** Set the loaf, still in the pan, on a wire cooling rack. Let it cool for 10 minutes — this helps the loaf solidify and makes it easier to remove from the pan.
- **Remove from pan and cool another 10 minutes.** Grasping the parchment paper sling, lift the loaf out of the pan and place on the cooling rack. Cool for another 10 minutes before slicing.
- Great served with ice cream or as a breakfast treat

———————————————

Late Night Treat
Dry your eyes with a
no bake ugly cookies

Ingredients

2cups sugar
1/4 cup brown sugar (Optional)
1/2 cup milk
1 stick (8 tablespoons) unsalted butter
1/4 cup unsweetened cocoa powder
3 cups old-fashioned rolled oats
1 cup crunchy peanut butter
1 tablespoon pure vanilla extract
Large pinch kosher salt

Line a baking sheet with wax paper or parchment.
Bring the sugar, milk, butter and cocoa to a boil in a medium saucepan over medium heat, stirring occasionally, then let boil for 1 minute. Remove from the heat. Add the oats, peanut butter, vanilla and salt, and stir to combine.
Drop teaspoonfuls of the mixture onto the prepared baking sheet, and let sit at room temperature until cooled and hardened, about 30 minutes. Refrigerate in an airtight container for up to 3 days.

———————————————

These dishes have been passed down and around through our family for years some traditional some not so much
No matter the occasion
they have been a familiar ice breaker helped us get through-some of the hardest dinners of are life I pray you find some comfort in what we consider -soul food -

Counseling for Grieving Couples & Families

Both separately and collectively, my family and friends needed help processing the loss of our son, brother, uncle, cousin, and friend, our well-loved Anthony Jr, AJ, Bone and JReal.

He was someone different in each of our lives. We tried to comfort each other, but the energy transfer was at too high of a voltage or the charger was too damaged to help each other keep a healthy conversation going. There was nothing more important than staying close to one another in this difficult time. Before we accepted help, we would just wing it, whatever the atmosphere provided. We would follow suit even if we would remain the whole day mourning like mute zombies. Literally walking around dying on the inside.

Finally, we accepted help from Hospice through their Sudden Death and Homicide Program, sponsored by the Metro Government and Police Department.

We attended their grief counseling sessions that same year. In August 2015, we participated in weekend grief camp.

We have attended several of the annual memorial services in March, the month of AJ's birth. I have even returned as the Guest Speaker of 2017.

If I have to give a mourning family advice, it is to get help mentally, physically, and spiritually. I promise, it will make the mending process so much better

Counseling Sessions and Services

OASIS Retreat and Wellness Center
Yvonne McCoy
205 Townepark Circle Suite 100
Louisville, Kentucky 40243
(502) 664-0373

Creative Spirits Behavior Health Inc.
Cassandra Gray
12730 Townepark Way, Suite 201
Louisville, KY 40243
502-254-9555

Revelation Counseling Center
LaShonda Fletcher
4333 S. Brook St.
Louisville, KY 40214
502-224-4478

Brittany A. Johnson LMHC
Brittany Johnson
727 Mt. Tabor Rd, Suite C,
New Albany, IN 47150
(502) 744-2460

Crimson Dove Counseling Services
Main Office
214 Breckenridge Ln

Suite #203
Louisville, KY 40207
Perry Blair
(502) 742-4014
crimsondovecounseling@gmail.com

Franklin Office
127 Memorial Dr.,
Franklin, KY 42134
(270) 253-3538
crimsondovefranklin@gmail.com

Reflection

Do you remember the story of Jonah? (Jonah chapter 1-4)....#flashbackmemory

I've been trying to post this message for 2 days now and for some reason I would get sad .....side tracked or my phone would go dead but it's been pressing on my heart to share. So, I guess I'll start with this Mother's heart.

We are Our children's first teachers and we teach them what we think is important to know........

From an early age, I instilled prayer & a understanding of who God (is) into to my children. A relationship with Christ is a must in our household.

However, as our life adjusts to the loss of our son AJ, we are going through his belongings deciding things to keep & throw away etc.

I have pretty much avoided this task since his death. Well it was pressing on me to make sure my husband packed away everything I requested that I wanted to keep. Well, long story short, that meant that I had to go check the room over myself ......smh....Well, while I was down there I just took my time to inhale the faint smell of him...... in the air. I sat on his bed and just cried....knowing & feeling that he truly is gone.....this is no longer his home/room ....I began to talk to the Lord and as I called out AJ's name. I got up & went over to his dresser drawer and this is what I found.

Wow...............my lord what a surprise and a sign to me that he is with the Lord .....For the Bible I instilled in him was the word he hid in his heart this book is over 10 years old. Apparently this Bible moved with us all down through the years. He could have lost it or thrown it away but it was with his keepsakes....What can I say but thank you Jesus .....#truly the Word of God says, "to train up a child in the way he should go and when he's older that he wouldn't depart from it." I believe God and I trust his word .#to be absent from this mortal body is to be present with the Lord and I'm ecstatic about that. I choose to celebrate your life !!!!!!!

I'm learning to understand the Master's plan

Reflection

Your Loved Ones Belongings and Inventory

What to do with your child's belongings.

Make three labeled groups:

-Keepsake

-Pass down

-Donate

Keepsakes- these are the items you simply can't part with. They hold special sentimental value and significance. This may include things with your child's unique scent on them, such as a favorite toy, book, or a special article of clothing. Include favorites you loved to see them wear. Maybe a jersey, hat, hair bow, memorabilia, or items with their initials or name on them.

Pass down -all the things that hold less sentimental value, but are still in good shape and condition to pass down to others. Pass them to another child in the family, daycare or school resource center they once attended.

Donate- to Goodwill, Salvation Army, group homes, shelters, and/or large families. Furniture, electronics or unused toiletries, like diapers, formula, wipes are examples of welcomed items used to bless others.

What to do on your child's birthday, Christmas, or major events, when you would want to include them?

I celebrate AJ's birthday every year. In his memory I order a cake, buy a gift and either keep it or donate it to a child with the same birthday.

On Christmas, I deliver what I affectionately call, "AJ's gifts." On behalf of AJ, I shop, wrap and give these special items. I label a gift for each family member as, "A gift from heaven, from our beloved AJ." It is fair to say that everyone looks forward to "AJ gifts." We laugh, recount special stories, as I tell why AJ would have bought this particular gift for them. This is a way of keeping your loved one present in your life.

When we do large family events, we bring a framed portrait of AJ along because he is forever a staple part of our family.

Turn your pain into power. Find something to lend your support to and stay faithful to doing it. Learn to give out of your need. Do you need strength? Help someone that may be physically weak, like an elderly person. Do you need compassion? Do random acts of kindness. If you need support, offer your support to others.

*Acts 20:35 - New International Version

In everything I did, I showed you that by this kind of hard work we must help the weak, remembering the words the Lord Jesus himself said: 'It is more blessed to give than to receive.'

Attitude of Gratitude

"Gratitude; my cup overfloweth."— Anonymous

"Gratitude, like faith, is a muscle. The more you use it, the stronger it grows, and the more power you have to use it on your behalf. If you do not practice gratefulness, its benefaction will go unnoticed, and your capacity to draw on its gifts will be diminished. To be grateful is to find blessings in everything. This is the most powerful attitude to adopt, for there are blessings in everything."— Alan Cohen

Gratitude words so you can practice and remain grateful for the people/things and relationship that you still have that support you and remain.

Show gratitude through grief.... these sentences belong to someone in your life that has walked with you on this grief journey.

Feel free to use the following sentences to help you find the words for the thank you cards to express your gratitude, thankfulness and appreciation.

1. How can we ever thank you enough for all you've done? We're forever grateful.
2. You helped me right when I needed help most.
3. If anyone deserves thanks, it's you.
4. I really appreciate your support in this endeavor.
5. You have been extremely supportive through this difficult time.
6. I could not have gotten through it without you.
7. We must thank you for your support at this time.

8. I want to thank you for all the support and concern.

9. That was very kind of you.

10. How can I ever repay you? Your support has made me a stronger person and I will forever be grateful.

11. You're my best friend. Thank you for always being there for me.

12. Taking the time to help me was a very nice thing for you to do.

13. Thanks so much.

14. Thank you for thinking of me and taking the time to be kind.

15. You are the most beautiful and wonderful thing that has ever happened to me. I'm so lucky!

12-Month Plan of Scriptural Inspiration and Motivation

Death is so immediate, tragic and overwhelming that you have to find ways to stay encouraged each and every day.

Utilize this 12 Month, 365 day scriptural guide to help you along this grieving journey each and every day of the year.

"Thy word is a lamp unto my feet and a light unto my pathway."
Psalm 119:105 (KJV)

JANUARY

DAY 1: ECCLESIASTES 3:11
DAY 2: ISAIAH 40:31
DAY 3: JEREMIAH 29:11
DAY 4: JOB 8:7
DAY 5: PHILIPPIANS 3:13, 14
DAY 6: ISAIAH 43:18. 19
DAY 7: LAMENTATIONS 3:22, 23
DAY 8: EPHESIANS 4:22-24
DAY 9: 2 CORINTHIANS 5:17
DAY 10: PSALM 40:3
DAY 11: EZEKIEL 11:19
DAY 12: MATTHEW 26:27-29
DAY 13: ISAIAH 65:17
DAY 14: ROMANS 6:4
DAY 15: COLOSSIANS 3:9-10
DAY 16: REVELATION 21:5
DAY 17: ACTS 3:19
DAY 18: 2 CHRONICLES 7:14
DAY 19: EZEKIEL 36:26
DAY 20: ISAIAH 58:12
DAY 21: HEBREWS 12:1, 2
DAY 22: 1 PETER 1:23
DAY 23: HEBREWS 4:16
DAY 24: ROMANS 12:2
DAY 25: MATTHEW 7:7, 8
DAY 26: JOHN 10:10
DAY 27: PHILIPPIANS 4:6, 7
DAY 28: GALATIANS 6:14-16
DAY 29: PSALM 98:1-3
DAY 30: 1 PETER 1:3
DAY 31: 1 JOHN 2:17

Reflection

FEBRUARY

DAY 1:   MARK 11:25
DAY 2: LUKE 17:4
DAY 3: EPHESIANS 4:32
DAY 4: COLOSSIANS 3:13
DAY 5: PROVERBS 3:3
DAY 6: MATTHEW 5:7
DAY 7: LUKE 6:36
DAY 8: MATTHEW 18:21-35
DAY 9: 1 JOHN 1:9
DAY 10: ISAIAH 1:18
DAY 11: MATTHEW 6:14, 15
DAY 12: EPHESIANS 1:7
DAY 13: COLOSSIANS 1:13, 14
DAY 14: PSALM 103:12
DAY 15: 2 CORINTHIANS 2:5-8
DAY 16: ACTS 7:59, 60
DAY 17: ROMANS 12:20
DAY 18: PSALM 130:3, 4
DAY 19: ISAIAH 43:25
DAY 20: MICAH 7:18, 19
DAY 21: LUKE 7:47, 48
DAY 22: ACTS 3:19
DAY 23: 1 JOHN 2:1, 2
DAY 24: 1 PETER 3:9
DAY 25: JAMES 5:16
DAY 26: PROVERBS 15:18
DAY 27: PROVERBS 17:9
DAY 28: PSALM 86:5

Reflection

#flashbackmemory #fiveyearmemory - Feb 16, 2015 exactly 3 months ago yesterday we laid our son Anthony Jr. to rest. It's been the longest 90days in our life ....I want to take this time to express to all the people who have supported & shown us love in our time of sorrow .....

We truly appreciate you.(It's sad to say) but.....No one can really understand until you've had to walk in a pair of (Reality) shoes that you wished didn't fit........

It's so uncomfortable & confusing watching everything about our son's case be told to us only through the media and having the most painful time of your life be on public display ....Everywhere we go and anything we do, we live in a constant reminder of his death......It's so hard to just breathe at times .....When I say it's a heaviness that can deplete you ....If we/I weren't believers, I would have given up by now! Trust.......(I'm not doing this in my own strength)

It's so true y'all, the enemies' plan is to kill steal & destroy ..... #but God) We are holding tight to his unchanging hand, putting all our faith and trust in Him. He's the same God that has been there through every other hardship in our life's. Even though this is the most testing trail in our life. We have chosen to trust the Lord FB family & friends. We are in need of your help once again

please if you will 🙏🙏🙏🙏🙏 for the next (30) days. Will you remember to call out the Smith's (AJ) name in your prayers. We need a favorable outcome & a peaceful closure for our son & family (justice). This would be a great start to our healing process. (I need every believer) to agree we me that #God will get the glory out of this. Amen!

P.S. Thanks in advance

Reflection

MARCH

DAY 1: LUKE 17:5
DAY 2: ROMANS 10:17
DAY 3: GALATIANS 5:6
DAY 4: HEBREWS 11:1
DAY 5: JAMES 2:17
DAY 6: 1 JOHN 5:4, 5
DAY 7: JOHN 6:29
DAY 8: HEBREWS 11:6
DAY 9: JAMES 1:6
DAY 10: PSALM 37:5
DAY 11: PROVERBS 3:5
DAY 12: MATTHEW 6:30
DAY 13: MATTHEW 17:20
DAY 14: 2 CORINTHIANS 5:7
DAY 15: ACTS 26:18
DAY 16: EPHESIANS 6:16
DAY 17: 2 TIMOTHY 4:7
DAY 18: MATTHEW 14:29-31
DAY 19: JOHN 20:29
DAY 20: 1 JOHN 5:13
DAY 21: GALATIANS 3:22
DAY 22: JOHN 1:12
DAY 23: MARK 10:52
DAY 24: ROMANS 1:17
DAY 25: 1 PETER 1:21
DAY 26: TITUS 1:2
DAY 27: 1 CORINTHIANS 16:13
DAY 28: MARK 11:24
DAY 29: 1 TIMOTHY 6:11
DAY 30: 1 THESSALONIANS 1:3
DAY 31: 1 PETER 1:7

Reflection

APRIL

DAY 1: PHILIPPIANS 4:6, 7
DAY 2: MATTHEW 11:28-30
DAY 3: JOHN 14:27
DAY 4: PROVERBS 12:25
DAY 5: PSALM 55:22
DAY 6: 1 PETER 5:6-8
DAY 7: HEBREWS 13:5, 6
DAY 8: PSALM 56:3
DAY 9: PSALM 23:1, 2
DAY 10: PROVERBS 3:5, 6
DAY 11: ROMANS 8:38, 39
DAY 12: COLOSSIANS 3:15
DAY 13: 2 THESSALONIANS 3:16
DAY 14: PSALM 23:4
DAY 15: ISAIAH 41:10
DAY 16: 2 TIMOTHY 1:7
DAY 17: 1 JOHN 4:18
DAY 18: PSALM 94:19
DAY 19: ISAIAH 43:1
DAY 20: JOSHUA 1:9
DAY 21: MATTHEW 6:34
DAY 22: LUKE 12:22-26
DAY 23: PSALM 27:1
DAY 24: MARK 6:5
DAY 25: DEUTERONOMY 31:6
DAY 26: PSALM 46:1
DAY 27: PSALM 118:6, 7
DAY 28: 1 PETER 3:14
DAY 29: MARK 5:36
DAY 30: REVELATION 1:17

Reflection

MAY

DAY 1: MATTHEW 11:28-30
DAY 2: PSALM 73:26
DAY 3: JOHN 14:27
DAY 4: PSALM 55:22
DAY 5: 1 PETER 4:19
DAY 6: 2 CORINTHIANS 5:6, 7
DAY 7: PSALM 147:3
DAY 8: 1 PETER 5:7
DAY 9: ISAIAH 40:31
DAY 10: LUKE 10:41, 42
DAY 11: NEHEMIAH 8:10
DAY 12: JOHN 16:33
DAY 13: PSALM 4:8
DAY 14: EXODUS 33:14
DAY 15: PSALM 121:1-3
DAY 16: JEREMIAH 31:25
DAY 17: HEBREWS 12:12, 13
DAY 18: COLOSSIANS 1:29
DAY 19: GALATIANS 6:9
DAY 20: PROVERBS 3:24
DAY 21: PSALM 46:10
DAY 22: JOHN 16:24
DAY 23: ISAIAH 26:3
DAY 24: HEBREWS 4:16
DAY 25: PSALM 55:6
DAY 26: PROVERBS 23:23, 24
DAY 27: PSALM 18:31, 32
DAY 28: JAMES 1:12
DAY 29: REVELATION 2:3
DAY 30: HEBREWS 6:10
DAY 31: ISAIAH 55:11

Reflection

JUNE

DAY 1: ROMANS 8:15
DAY 2: ISAIAH 41:10
DAY 3: 1 JOHN 4:18, 19
DAY 4: JOSHUA 1:9
DAY 5: PSALM 23:4
DAY 6: JOHN 14:27
DAY 7: PSALM 27:1
DAY 8: ISAIAH 43:1
DAY 9: DEUTERONOMY 31:6
DAY 10: 1 CORINTHIANS 16:13
DAY 11: HEBREWS 13:6
DAY 12: PSALM 34:4
DAY 13: PSALM 118:6
DAY 14: ISAIAH 41:13
DAY 15: 1 PETER 3:14
DAY 16: 2 TIMOTHY 1:6
DAY 17: PSALM 56:3, 4
DAY 18: PROVERBS 12:25
DAY 19: MATTHEW 6:34
DAY 20: PSALM 55:22
DAY 21: ROMANS 8:38, 39
DAY 22: PSALM 27:3
DAY 23: MARK 5:36
DAY 24: PROVERBS 29:25
DAY 25: PSALM 94:19
DAY 26: ISAIAH 26:3
DAY 27: PROVERBS 3:5
DAY 28: PSALM 91:7
DAY 29: ISAIAH 35:4
DAY 30: PSALM 112:7

Reflection

JULY

DAY 1: ISAIAH 40:29-31
DAY 2: EXODUS 14:14
DAY 3: 2 CHRONICLES 7:14
DAY 4: JAMES 1:5
DAY 5: PHILIPPIANS 4:19
DAY 6: PSALM 37:4
DAY 7: JOHN 14:13-16
DAY 8: LUKE 11:9-13
DAY 9: MATTHEW 6:31-33
DAY 10: PROVERBS 3:5, 6
DAY 11: ROMANS 10:9, 10
DAY 12: REVELATION 3:5
DAY 13: JOHN 8:36
DAY 14: DEUTERONOMY 31:8
DAY 15: JAMES 4:7
DAY 16: ISAIAH 61:1
DAY 17: ISAIAH 54:17
DAY 18: 1 PETER 4:1, 2
DAY 19: 2 CORINTHIANS 4:17, 18
DAY 20: COLOSSIANS 3:3, 4
DAY 21: REVELATION 2:7
DAY 22: ISAIAH 43:2
DAY 23: JOHN 3:36
DAY 24: MALACHI 3:10
DAY 25: PSALM 18:3
DAY 26: EPHESIANS 3:16-19
DAY 27: PSALM 103:2-5
DAY 28: 2 SAMUEL 7:28
DAY 29: PSALM 19:7
DAY 30: JOHN 10:10
DAY 31: ISAIAH 54:10

Reflection

AUGUST

DAY 1: PSALM 42:5
DAY 2: JEREMIAH 31:3
DAY 3: PSALM 34:8
DAY 4: ISAIAH 54:10
DAY 5: ZEPHANIAH 3:17
DAY 6: ROMANS 8:37
DAY 7: PSALM 42:11
DAY 8: JOHN 16:33
DAY 9: PSALM 147:3
DAY 10: 2 THESSALONIANS 3:5
DAY 11: JOB 22:29
DAY 12: PSALM 40:1-3
DAY 13: PSALM 3:3
DAY 14: MATTHEW 11:28,29
DAY 15: PSALM 23:4
DAY 16: 1 PETER 5:7
DAY 17: PSALM 30:11
DAY 18: 2 TIMOTHY 1:7
DAY 19: PROVERBS 12:25
DAY 20: DEUTERONOMY 33:27A
DAY 21: 2 CORINTHIANS 1:3, 4
DAY 22: ISAIAH 41:10
DAY 23: ROMANS 8:38, 39
DAY 24: PSALM 9:9
DAY 25: PROVERBS 15:13
DAY 26: ISAIAH 42:3
DAY 27: ECCLESIASTES 9:7
DAY 28: 2 CORINTHIANS 4:7-10
DAY 29: JAMES 5:13
DAY 30: 1 PETER 4:14
DAY 31: DEUTERONOMY 31:8

Reflection

SEPTEMBER

DAY 1: ECCLESIASTES 3:11
DAY 2: PSALM 27:14
DAY 3: LUKE 1:45
DAY 4: 1 SAMUEL 12:16
DAY 5: ISAIAH 40:31
DAY 6: PSALM 37:7
DAY 7: JOHN 13:7
DAY 8: PHILIPPIANS 1:6
DAY 9: EXODUS 14:14
DAY 10: HEBREWS 6:15
DAY 11: MICAH 7:7
DAY 12: ROMANS 12:12
DAY 13: COLOSSIANS 1:11
DAY 14: 1 CORINTHIANS 15:58
DAY 15: JAMES 5:11
DAY 16: LAMENTATIONS 3:25
DAY 17: ISAIAH 30:18
DAY 18: JAMES 1:12
DAY 19: PSALM 40:1,2
DAY 20: PSALM 62:5
DAY 21: ACTS 1:4
DAY 22: GALATIANS 6:9
DAY 23: 2 PETER 3:9
DAY 24: PSALM 33:20
DAY 25: PSALM 130:5
DAY 26: PSALM 31:14, 15
DAY 27: PSALM 62:7, 8
DAY 28: ISAIAH 58:11
DAY 29: ISAIAH 33:2
DAY 30: JAMES 5:7

Reflection

OCTOBER

DAY 1: DANIEL 2:20
DAY 2: JOHN 4:2
DAY 3: PSALM 22:27
DAY 4: PSALM 29:2
DAY 5: PSALM 66:4
DAY 6: PSALM 95:6
DAY 7: PSALM 96:9
DAY 8: PSALM 99:5
DAY 9: PSALM 138:2
DAY 10: JEREMIAH 7:2
DAY 11: PSALM 34:3
DAY 12: PSALM 69:30
DAY 13: LUKE 1:46
DAY 14: PSALM 22:22
DAY 15: PSALM 27:6
DAY 16: PSALM 33:2
DAY 17: PSALM 34:1
DAY 18: PSALM 35:8
DAY 19: PSALM 40:3
DAY 20: PSALM 42:5
DAY 21: PSALM 44:8
DAY 22: PSALM 47:6
DAY 23: ACTS 16:25
DAY 24: ROMANS 15:11
DAY 25: EPHESIANS 1:6
DAY 26: HEBREWS 2:12
DAY 27: HEBREWS 13:15
DAY 28: 1 PETER 2:9
DAY 29: PSALM 68:4
DAY 30: PSALM 69:34
DAY 31: PSALM 71:8

Reflection

NOVEMBER

DAY 1: PSALM 50:14
DAY 2: COLOSSIANS 4:2
DAY 3: EZRA 3:11
DAY 4: PSALM 140:13
DAY 5: 2 CORINTHIANS 4:15
DAY 6: 2 SAMUEL 22:50
DAY 7: 2 CORINTHIANS 9:15
DAY 8: PSALM 26:6, 7
DAY 10: DANIEL 6:10
DAY 11: PSALM 136:2
DAY 12: MATTHEW 26:27
DAY 13: 1 TIMOTHY 4:4
DAY 14: ROMANS 14:6
DAY 15: PSALM 69:30
DAY 16: EPHESIANS 1:16
DAY 17: 1 CHRONICLES 16:8
DAY 18: COLOSSIANS 1:3
DAY 19: JONAH 2:9
DAY 20: PSALM 18:49
DAY 21: 1 CORINTHIANS 15:57
DAY 22: ROMANS 16:4
DAY 23: PSALM 100:4
DAY 24: 1 THESSALONIANS 5:18
DAY 25: PSALM 35:18
DAY 26: 2 CORINTHIANS 2:14
DAY 27: REVELATION 7:12
DAY 28: PSALM 30:4
DAY 29: 1 CHRONICLES 16:34
DAY 30: PSALM 116:17

Reflection

DECEMBER

DAY 1: ROMANS 13:8
DAY 2: MATTHEW 5:43-48
DAY 3: JOHN 13:34, 35
DAY 4: 1 PETER 4:8
DAY 5: ROMANS 12:10
DAY 6: LEVITICUS 19:18
DAY 7: PROVERBS 17:17
DAY 8: 1 CORINTHIANS 16:14
DAY 9: 1 JOHN 4:18, 19
DAY 10: LUKE 6:25
DAY 11: PROVERBS 10:12
DAY 12: EPHESIANS 4:32
DAY 13: 1 JOHN 4:11
DAY 14: COLOSSIANS 3:14
DAY 15: MARK 12:31
DAY 16: 1 THESSALONIANS 4:9
DAY 17: JAMES 1:27
DAY 18: LUKE 6:27, 28
DAY 19: GALATIANS 5:14
DAY 20: JOHN 15:9
DAY 21: 1 CORINTHIANS 13:1, 2
DAY 22: EPHESIANS 5:2
DAY 23: GALATIANS 6:2
DAY 24: LUKE 3:11
DAY 25: JOHN 15:13
DAY 26: HEBREWS 13:1, 2
DAY 27: DEUTERONOMY 15:11
DAY 28: RUTH 1:16, 17
DAY 29: ROMANS 12:9-16
DAY 30: 1 JOHN 4:7, 8
DAY 31: LUKE 6:32

Reflection

Reflection

Activities

Growing Through Year 1

Write your future self a letter and date it a year from now.

Reflection

Growing Through Year 3

Compare yourself from Year 1 to Year 3 – How much have you have you grown? How much have you sown? Sow your way out of grief.

Reflection

Growing Through Year 5

How have you established to commemorate your child's legacy? What have you done in their memory to create a legacy? Are there any organizations, events, foundations that you partner with that is a testament to their legacy?

Year 5 Reflection

Liked by **settinmeup**, **_coco_payne_** and **14 others**

blackbeautiful1 I know its the reflection from the sun , but I choose to believe you where getting fitted for your angel wings that day ..... only God knows a man's heart
 and the plan for there life.
I know with out question I will forever carry you in my spirit
your my first love 2/7/15 a part of me died with you however I'm going to use my life to keep you alive I choose to celebrate your life and not mourn your death .....
the lord being my strength me an the family will carry out all your dreams and goals keep watching from heaven you'll see # justice & your dreams coming true I've written everything we talked about down I cherish those plans....smh I love you back to life everyday rest now baby mama & daddy got your back & that's a fact!💔7months 9/7/15

SEPTEMBER 7, 2015

References and Resources

https://www.funeralbasics.org/write-great-obituary/ - How to Write an Obituary.

https://dying.lovetoknow.com/How_Do_I_Write_a_Funeral_Program - How do I write a funeral program?

When AJ first died, I couldn't sleep, I didn't want to eat and had no one to talk to, adult coloring sheets and doodling brought me so much peace. I trust that they will bring you peace as well.
Get your free copies at www.art-is-fun.com/free-adult-coloring-pages

A gift for you and your future. Create or update your will today – Fast and 100% free http://www.freewill.com

Books

Here are some books that helped me as a grieving Christian and Married Mourning Mother.

Almost Divorced: Marriage Is Hard Work Duuuhhh

Jackie Archie

I wasn't ready to say goodbye

Authors Brook Noel and Pamela D. Blair, Ph.D., offer a comforting hand to hold for those who are grieving the sudden death of a loved one.

Hugs from Heaven

About the author - Caron Chandler Loveless is a bestselling author, artist, life coach, and co-host of The Live True Podcast.

One Marriage under God

Robert Noland foreword by Darren and Heather Turner

It's OK That You're Not OK

Meeting Grief and Loss in a Culture That Doesn't Understand

By: Megan Devine and Narrated by: Megan Devine

Categories: Health & Wellness, Psychology & Mental Health

Hope for the Brokenhearted: God's Voice of Comfort in the Midst of Grief and Loss

John Luke Terveen - January 1, 2006 David C Cook

TARC (Transit Authority of the River City)

The Beauty and Health Industry for their support

Louisville Metro Police Department. Thank you from Anthony Smith

Tribute to Hosparice – August Evergreen Grief Camp
This free, one day camp is designed for families with children (age 6-18) who have experienced the death of a loved one. This virtual event will combine fun activities with important grief education and support sessions.

Evergreen activities/support will be directed by professional counselors with Hosparus Health Grief Counseling Center. Apply for admission by calling 502-456-5451. Evergreen is made possible through the generous support of the WHAS Crusade for Children and Kosair Charities, as well as other corporations, groups and individuals. Registration fees cover only a portion of the expense of this program.

Praise Covenant Louisville, KY | Bishop William Harris, Pastor

3107 Crums Lane, Louisville, KY

Pictorial Reflections

Liked by _coco_payne_, revdrwilson and 22 others
blackbeautiful1 It's been 5 months since I heard your voice seen your face kissed your forehead or had you here to wrap your arms around me & say mama I love you 🥺😭 I miss everything about you son my 1st born love # I will cherish this hug for the rest of my life 2/7/15 my heart stopped beating the same 💔 7/7/15....... Sip baby 😶😘

View 1 comment

JULY 7, 2015

Lanyia Smith
Mar 14, 2015

The pass month has felt so empty without you. Just know bubby you will never be forgotten. 💜🔒✊ — with **Elgina Latoya Smith.**

👍❤ 78   1 Comment

Elgina Latoya Smith is with **Angela StillSmiling.**
Mar 5, 2017 · Jeffersontown

Today has been truly a God sent conformation.....pain into empowering shifting into my purpose &devinePosition I can't quit #im unstoppable

 Elgina Latoya Smith is with **Anthony Smith.**
Feb 12, 2017

I just wanted to encourage someone's heart on tonight & give the devil a big fat black eye..... 2years ago I didn't own this smile and at the time I thought I'd never smile again after the death of my son...... (but God).....4years ago around this very same time I was fighting for m... See More

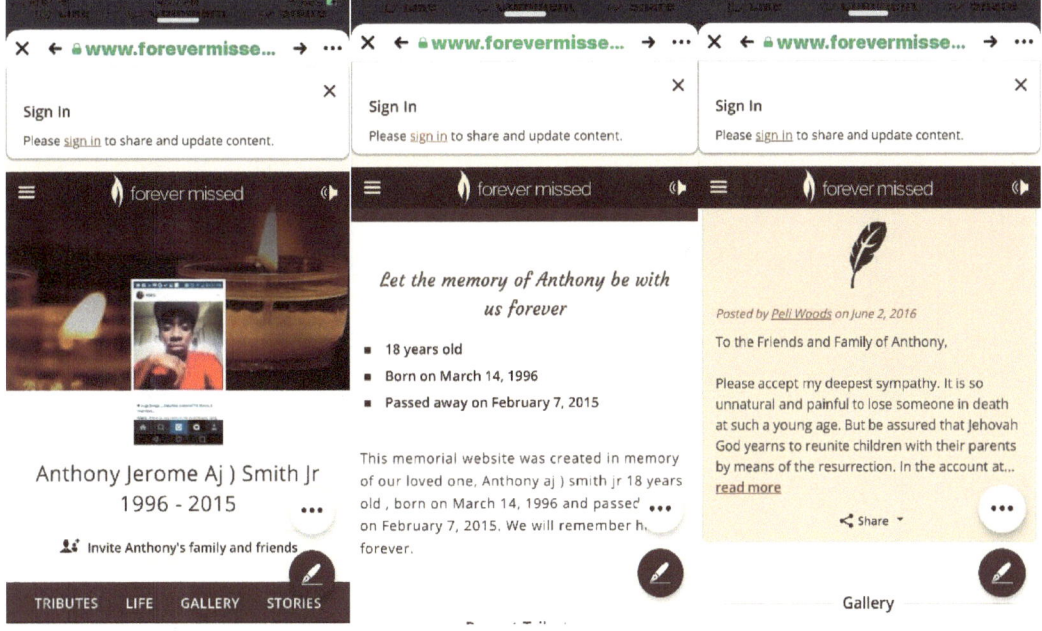

Liked by tamalametcalf, tvkia and 10 others
blackbeautiful1 Today God smiled on me. ....I was able to do something in honor of my son (Louisville biggest fan) .... I Went to have Breakfast at wild eggs this morning and who did I see I was blessed to meet russ 1 of Aj favorites and he even give me his autograph I did it for you son i know your happy! It will be a keepsake thanks again russ #you made my broken 💔 smike 😇
FEBRUARY 10, 2016

Reflection

Reflection

Reflection

Reflection

Reflection

Reflection

Reflection

Reflection

Reflection

Reflection

www.ingramcontent.com/pod-product-compliance
Lightning Source LLC
Chambersburg PA
CBHW041532220426
43662CB00002B/40